FIFTY POEMS FIFTY

by

REED WHITTEMORE

UNIVERSITY OF MINNESOTA PRESS, MINNEAPOLIS

Some of these poems first appeared in the *New Republic*, the *Virginia Quarterly Review*, the *Washington Post*, *Dryad*, the *Carleton Miscellany*, and *Voyages*.

TO HELEN

TABLE OF CONTENTS

FIFTY POEMS FIFTY

Baby girl, you have insomnia.
I know. I am forty-nine times your age.
   I have insomnia.
It brings us together.

In there, what are you thinking?
Softly you woof woof, like the neighbor's dog.
Gently your feet pound the crib, like the
   moon's hammers.
And now you are humming.
But what are you thinking?

In here, I, forty-niner, your comrade,
Am thinking darkly of moons and worlds
   and flesh,
As old sleepless ones do, softly.
Do you have dark thoughts?

I wish I could ask you, and hear your reply,
In there,
The two of us close and soft, far from the day.
But if I went in you would tease,
And not say.

My room overlooks the park.
The trees are like barbed wire.
My keepers are friendly but firm.
I am safe here.

Upright in bed mechanical,
Having bent to the temperature taker,
I await the tray lunch
Cooked by my maker.

My blood is in vats at the lab,
Also my urine.
My pills will appear at three.
X-ray wants me.

Am I deserving? No matter.
In shift serene I give thanks
For roses and mums
And respirator.

Let there be joy amid interns,
Let cashiers dance,
That I may further the work
And look at the park.

The bareness of the ground where the tent had been
    was testimony.
So too the miscellaneous childish junk thrown about. They
    had been there all right, and recently.
Nature would need a month maybe to restore the ground
    to middle-class sufficiency.
Meanwhile he walked the ground, picking up paper wrappers,
    taking stock, his own inventory of sufficiency.

"I have had a great sufficiency," he had to announce
    at the big round table,
Before his mother, presiding, would let him rise from
    his Bartlett pear and depart the parental twaddle.
Was it a joke? He never knew. He kept saying it.
    Now the table
Was his to preside at, having downed his new sufficiency,
    great or little,
Not pear only, not job, house, family, or future only,

Downed it and brought on the bash that bundled them off
    and gardened left him
With the small chores of seeding, watering, patiently
    practicing therapy
On a bare spot. He prayed for all their sufficiency.

Why do the children shout?
Something to shout about?
I search for a reason:
It's shouting season.

One has a megaphone.
"Abandon ship. We go down,"
He caws from his crow's nest,
And calls for the neighborhood life vest.

True, we are going down.
We are awash. We will drown.
But since he is busy playing
I am busy not saying.

Tell a boy he is a prophet?
I frown. I tell him to stop it.

Despite them, soon after birth, he gave up romance
As too short. They kept after him.
They plotted tedious beginnings and sticky middles,
With love hiding its sticky truths behind horses.
They pummeled and fractured poor tenderness
    for him, that sweetly
Its mending would serve as ending,
With Tchaikovski sawing the chapel up into fiddles.
But when they were done he was only fifteen,
    starting smoking.
Unreal.

They switched genres.
They started a war and took him and put
    him in jeeps
On real deserts,
With foulness bartering oranges at
    his fenders
While choruses chanted that this time
    was this one thus,
And for keeps.
Yet he wandered from Kitsch to Niente, and
    when the war ended
He was young yet and still splendid.
Unreal.

So they posted him back to where he began
    with his medals
To meet their ace reaper, the horrid
    sleepwalking creeper,

Who shoved him at desks, glued him to
    chairs and cares,
Bottled him up and cast him out on gray hours,
Where he bobbled and rolled and began to
    look stupid and old.
Real.

So he wrote his will,
And sickened, and jumped into bed, and looked
    suitably pale,
Chirping, "Ripeness is all."
Real.

Then they muffed it.
They muffed it by traipsing in healthy and
    dapper and drab,
Sniffling and snuffling, holding his hand
    in the cupola,
Gurgling how very, how too so, and
    fondling his flab.
They muffed it, and so he rose up, and
    removed his pajama,
And glowered at them, and swore, and
    turned on his sod,
And swept out the stained glass window
    to his God.
His.

In good ole day ze king need no committee.

Was nize.

Him says, them does; him sells, them buys.

Good system.

But then come big push make king one of guys.

So king buy chairs, say me no king me chairman.

So knocked off paradize.

Drab is the day in the uptown branch of the
    Middletown Public Library.
The bright cover colors for National Library Week
Have been filed away under "Colors for National Library Week."
Miss Prunewhip at the main desk is looking more and more
Like the 1928 edition of the Periodical Guide.
Yet it is outside the uptown branch that the
    inside has died.

It is outside where they have killed Miss Prunewhip,
    outside on the sidewalk.
Inside all is in order, magazines, books, periodicals
    all in order
(And if you put one out of order Miss Prunewhip will
    put on her glasses and whip you,
Orally of course, whip you, trip you, unzip you, and
    leave you bleeding in front of the circulation desk,
And morally of course,
Because Miss Prunewhip herself is certainly in order,
    and strong as a horse).

But outside on the sidewalk, under the trees, by the curb
All is not in order, not at all, not Prunewhip's order.
The leaves are not in order, and not on file; nor the faces,
No, the faces, in disorder, and the leaves, in disorder,
Swirl brazenly in the air, uncarded, unclassified.
It is outside Miss Prunewhip that the inside has died.

CABBY

"In all this mad
 Am I the only sane,"
 Thinks each mad cabby cruising the night-dazzle.

He dreams of rural meters ticking,
Grass streets.
He would end his Checkered career
In a bathysphere,
And peer through tinted glass at fish and coral,
Not men:
The cabby's moral.

11

So the baby chair overturned on the soft carpet,
And the baby herself, who had felled it,
   said it Fall Down.
Yes, yes, said I, Fall Down; and Boom, said she,
Happily, giving our love a bone.

I sat reading the paper.
She tiptoed off to the kitchen to implement Boom.
When she returned she was hitched.
   There was the story,
And picture too: baby and groom.

I put down the paper.
I righted the chair.
Dearest baby, wrote I in the wax weave
   of the carpet,
Why did you give your dada the air?

THE SET

The set was here last night.
They lounged in the living room in
   their minds and minis,
Chittering birds,
Bartering records and fashions so current
The ink was wet on their words.

I sat in a corner
Reading my Gutenberg.

The room was the same —
Curtains, calamities, lamps
All as they used to be
When they belonged to me.

DEATH

I read of the lords of death in old books:
Of the pyramids and pits
Into which they marched with their wives and
    best plates,
And lived dead but dressy in heaven nooks;

And of the slaves of death who naked marched
    to the pits
To serve those lords.
Dully they bowed and duly they lost their heads,
And slaved through in the bone as flowerpots.

A democrat myself I read my culture
As the first one to assert man's natural right
To die in his own way at his own rate,
So long as he slaves the dying of no other.

Now the real in the mind lives and reads the flesh,
And the flesh on the bone lives and reads the bone,
And the bone with the marrow lives, reading the marrow —
And none is lord but the lord death live in the marrow,
Holy illiterate, maker, spider of bone.

The mind wears many hats, many different wares.
Like a bird on a spit it turns in its living sleep.
It is quick, slow, open, secret, crammed with
    jokes, prayers.
It knows not what it knows deep.

Yet I have known one kind of mind whose vision
Is steady as the sphinx's, and whose mold
Is rock against all sea and salt and season.
Such a mind, soul, have the old.

They traffic in fixities; they sit in corners sipping.
In the sharp declivities of the times they
    save their breath.
They are more put out by a misplaced tool or letter
Than birth or death.

And when they talk they talk to themselves;
    their rhetoric
Wanders off into privacies where a word
Cares not who hears it, and eloquence
Is a canard.

I know a mind, soul, whose time now leads it
Shoreward to silence.
Not long ago it chattered like half a school,
And bade the desert dance.

The ads keep asking his help for the poor,
    the distressed,
The aged, the orphaned, the whatnot.
Now here is one asking him cleverly
    what he can do
For the earth's three hundred million
Illiterate.

He can burn books.

He is overextended.
He is bringing the peace already, and
    saving the ghetto.
He feels helpless.
He would ask *them* to help *him*, if they
    could read him.
He feels death far off and high, in
    open places.
Help! he is lying in orchards on
    steep slopes.
Help! he is bones, he is wind flesh.
    Send money,
Hope.

But the plight of the Indian.

And the whooping crane.

What avails?
He draws two gravely wounded bucks from
    his sad wallet
For Christmas Seals.

It was in a little backward country known as
    Backward Country
        That nestled (that was one of its troubles;
            it nestled)
        Between the Advanced Iron Works and the
            Lesser Spaceport —
It was on Wisdom Day in B.C. (which was a national
    holiday in B.C.)
        (As well as the Royal Philosopher's birthday)
        That the Royal Philosopher himself rolled
            from his cave
        At high noon,
        And announced to the Backward Press that
            since he was eighty,
        And since Wisdom Day was his day,
        The day was a good day to bring the citizenry
            up-to-date.
So it was on Wisdom Day that the citizenry heard
    their ragged sage relate,
        With his sour wit,
        The imminent death of their small state —
        From what?
        Ho ho, from dying.

           ✦   ✦   ✦

        Well! you can bet the news woke up the
            telegraph operator,
        And the seamstress who had been sewing
            the King's new clothes;

And jarred the Royal Abacus, and the
    Army and Navy,
And blew right out of his laboratory the
    phlogiston chemist.
Everybody was upset.
The streets filled quickly.
But the head of the Riot Commission said the
    situation would be met.

✔ ✔ ✔

Meanwhile the Royal Philosopher,
Having said what he had to say, and
    needing breakfast,
Rolled back in his cave, boiled six
    four-minute eggs,
Ate the eggs with his cavemate (the boy
    who cried wolf),
Cleaned up the dishes, put his dirty loin
    cloth in the washer, counted his gold,
And went back to bed to be comfortably
    dreamless and old.

✔ ✔ ✔

And the cobblestone asked of the curb,
Wherefore the hectic pace,
And the nervous creakings of limbs and
    minds in the marketplace?
And the curb replied to the cobblestone
That the people had suffered great loss
    in the forenoon.

"Was it a death?" "Not yet." "A fall
    in the marketplace?" "Not yet."

"Mayhap the young Prince was thrown
     from his horse?"
  The curb said it didn't know but thought
     it was worse.

"Then," roundly opined the cobblestone,
"It was the Royal Distillery. It burned down."

＜　＜　＜

But it was not the Royal Distillery, nor the Prince.
     No visible catastrophe had occurred; in fact
        the statistics
     From the Departments of Healthy Fixity and
        Orderly Vice
     Showed the day as pleasantly stagnant,
        meaning normal.
It was the minds, the minds only, that the gay old
  philosopher
     Had touched, but touched well;
     — Touched the Royal Artist,
     Who strode through the central square, his
        official thumb up,
     Sketching his subjects as sticks, with
        balloons from their mouths
     Ascending, saying, "End now," saying, "No more";
     — Touched the Culture Commission
     To proffer emergency medals
     To seven very dead poets for courageously
        staying so;
     — And touched the King,
     Who looked out his window idly at green,
        at blue,
     And felt himself drawn

To the nameless aimless where lost kings go.
So it was by evening, on Wisdom Day, that the words
    of the morning
        Had swept B.C. and beyond, leaving
        A premonitory gloom in the hearts of the faithful.
And it was by evening
        That many a burgher went sadly to packing his duffel.

✓ ✓ ✓

        Yes he went to packing
        He went to stashing the family treasures in
            rolled towels;
        He went to drawing money from banks,
            buying tickets, maps;
        He went to latching, locking, and zipping; he went
            to buckling down tarps,
        Only to pause, half done, and put it all back,
        And sit practicing patience, remembering
        That never a room could be had in the countries beyond
        For his kind.

✓ ✓ ✓

        And the cobblestone asked of the curb
        Wherefore at midnight a steady unseemly rumbling
        Filled air, and put earth to shaking.

        And the curb replied to the cobblestone
        That a fearfulness was occurring under the moon.

        "Was it a revolution?" "Could be." "An
            earthquake?" "Could be."
        "Mayhap the King has purchased a Sherman tank?"
        "More likely," deductively cobbled the stone in delight,
        "Militant youth is ranging the night."

It must have been nearly dawn when the Royal Philosopher
   Woke to the rumbling
   And rushed from his cave to be witness
   To bulldozers rolling,
   Leveling,
   Building a runway
   Athwart the valley.
It must have been later he came to the palace bearing his slingshot
   To waken the King:
   "Sire?"
   "Seer?"
   "Do you hear?"
   "I hear."
And it must have been later yet he returned to his cave
      And found there the boy who cried
         wolf, crying and crying,
   "Wolf."
      And the old philosopher said to him,
   "Those are not wolves, boy,
      Those are cats."

                    ✓   ✓   ✓

   Now engines whine through the valley
   Where the backwardness was,
   And travelers cluster in bars
   In the forwardness.

   The sage in his cave, the King in his palace
   And representative citizens in their original abodes
   May be seen from eleven to seven
   In the luxurious spaceport branch of
      Madame Tussaud's.

21

MONOLOGUE

I am warmer now.
Say I am warmer, more friendly.
The Evil One has slowly expelled Himself
Through my mouth and hands,
And now I am as if new from the shop,
My sweet self.
Say I am sweet.

Wasn't it dreadful
When I was puffed up like a blowfish
With Him?
How my gastrointestinal tract
Suffered! And my liver!
How I raged
(You may say I raged),
And paced and smoked,
Nights sleeplessly tossing,
Days seething.

Dreadful. But now He is gone.
Say He is gone.
He is gone and I am myself.
Where is my Evil One?

PRAYER

It may be that the Mayor will come down from
    his tower for the meeting.
It may be that the voters in their wisdom will
    sell the money tree.
But who will pound the gavel in the graveyard?
Be master, soul, master of our misery.

Let there be light in the darkroom, let freedom sting.
Bear the loaf and fish to Xerox and press
    the black button;
But choose from our most manifold resources
    some small wingding
To save sweet delicate poverty from the
    reformer glutton.

Yes, save our poverty, dear soul, save aches,
    save vice;
Save wretchedness, despair, save cancer, lice,
Lest the righteous go making day of the
    night of the wise,
And fire old Adam with napalm of paradise.

When politicos of the old life have departed,
Movers enter,
And painters,
And sometimes fumigators,
To help get the new life started.

In the halls there are boxes and echoes.
There is rain on windows.
Inside windows,
Framed by taxpayers' marble,
An occasional lingering face in its lostness mellows.

Newcomers straggle up and down in the wet,
Waiting in elegant duds on alien corners,
Calling for taxis,
Searching out parties,
Questing for something obscure, unnamed, unmet.

The something decided not to attend the Ball,
Nor grace the Parade.
It failed to appear and perform in the grandstand charade
On the Hill.
Maybe it hides in an old box in a hall?

Maybe not. Anyway, there are offices, empty.
There is rain.
There is marble.
There is also the rust and ruin of parting pleasantry —
There is also the new paint, in all the empty.

THE DRUG

Never will I write another sonnet
Now that Karl Shapiro's gone back on it.

It was igneous, it was basalt, it was
    a fierce fault;
It was eagles, or was it osprey? yes,
    it was love,
When in the gay gray Rockies of
    bibulous youth
My Edie and I communed and invented
    the cave.

The sun had shredded our shirts; our
    shoes grated.
We stood, in the gathering omens,
    graveled by Jove;
But rations we had, and lore, and
    sat scraping the lichen,
As our myriad passionate corpuscles
    crazied for cave.

Inward we scrabbled, tearing our nails
    and lorn flesh,
Bone against rock, soul-bone in each
    furious sleeve.
Brindled the night; the eyes of mountain
    cats mooned;
Yet we dug until it was dug, and swift
    dubbed it: cave.

Now here we lie luscious; with eagles we
    now here abide,
Having it made.

In spring into the world slips a we,
    but slithers
In autumn softly away as furnaces wake
To their hopeless war against
    cold-and-forever
Death in the dark for his dear sake

Who, that god of departures, dealt man,
    before he departed,
His final privacy.
So if one should ask for the music of
    midwinter Monday,
It is chuffing chimney,

And solo saunterings home in the
    snow's siftings
To Tuesday's dry die, Wednesday's deep
    dust and dwindle,
And days full three of bony disaster
    preceding
The final swindle

Known as Sunday. Oh day of rest,
Let the forlorn singular soul by the
    gone god, then, be blessed.

Who has the dream denied has the
   terror privilege
Admitting him unto the inner circle
   of souls
In hot veritas. The young are
   forbid there,
And the wise in their wastings like
   moles in foxy old holes

There hide, during drabs.
Them do not stir, sweet devil; to
   them let the real
Seep, and the sad earth's savings slide
And fill, and their feebles seal

Until firm,
That nobody nevered
Will rise from the depths then and
   jests savagely dangle
Where life and hope severed.

Who has the dream denied has the war won
Against all dirty deliverance under the sun.

GENESIS REVISED

"In my opinion this concept of the interval,
detached as it is from the selection of any special
body to occupy it, is the starting point of the
whole concept of space." — ALBERT EINSTEIN

Think of an "and" alone,
Nothing before, nothing after,
Nothing *and* nothing.
The "and" proposes a structure, and by the proposing
Is. And makes.
For nothing is nothing, but nothing *and* nothing
Are spatial, temporal; the structure does it,
A nothing there *and* here, a nothing then *and* now,
To and fro in the space-time.

But in grammar we cannot think of this. The
    "and" comes second.
We need something, *then* "and."
Or if we are willing to grant, without understanding,
    a precedent "and,"
We still ask to know where it came from.
Grammar, logic, math work in the matrix
Of the space-time. "And" is the space-time. We
    in its matrix
Know what we do in it, where we are in it,
But not it.

This that we don't know we call soul, spirit.
More of it every day is found in the physics lab,
By omission.
It is what we tend to describe by what it is not.

It is not logical; it is not metrical; it is not
    (as I now propose) grammatical.
Yet it is with us. Our minds seem made in its image,
Each a space-time kit for making a world up.
We cannot conceive of that spirit (the "and")
    as father,
Yet we cannot conceive of it otherwise. In
    Eddington's words,
The breach of causality keeps breaking the chain of
    inference. Sense leads to nonsense.

In the beginning, then, was nonsense? So every
    beginning. So far.
We cannot conceive of a nothing that makes something.
The "and" we say must be physical. Or electrical.
    Something.
Yet the something is nothing. Nonsense.
We have no grammar for nonsense; we cannot posit
A nothing-something moving between nothings.
Yet I repeat:
Think of an "and" alone,
Nothing before, nothing after,
Nothing *and* nothing, thereby making

The first day.

The iron garage is empty except for a few cardboard
    boxes filled with leaves and sticks.
It has no doors. At the end of a hilly alley it sits
    gaping at weeds, broken bottles, gravel.
It is poverty-stricken but resonant. Struck, it gives
    off a thunder sound, small thunder,
As when a baby anomie speaks its first consonant.
Where is the soul of an iron garage, where does
    it keep itself?
Soon the workers will come in a truck and haul
    the old hulk away.
Will the soul stay?

Garage soul, my soul goes out to you in your emptiness.
I too await the workers. You sit there, I here,
    dissidents adamantean.
Should we unite and make thunder against the full ones?

THE SILENT TEACHER IN THE DISAPPEARING CLASSROOM SHAGGY, WIZ NO BOOK

ON READING *The Disappearing Dais*, IN WHICH PROGRESSIVE EDUCATION COMES TO BRITISH SCHOOLS

A very long time ago, on the little ole isle of Popo,
    it was custom
For one big noisy guy to rent one big ole barn of hall
    and go to dustem
Chandeliers and highboys and purty ole madagascars, and
    wax ze parquet floor,
And put little brown desks in rows on floor, and
    big desk up before,
And knock up big black blackboard, and hangem picture
    of ze prexy
And ope ze window wide and tell ze world in sotto voce,
"School Day, School Day, Good ole Golden Rule Day!" —
    and ring ze bell,
And haul ze students in and givem heap big institutional
    cultural heritage hell.

So many many many many years went by wiz making big ole
    biz zis *profond* hell,
For which at eight each morn ze big guy tolled
    ze fearful bell,
And students sat there *glomp* as voice *grande* poured
    eternalle over,
And students wished *futilement* ze school days
    toute suite over,

And stick ze gum on seats,

Till happily ze wizard come *mit* goodies, *mit* sweets.

Ze wizard! Funny ole guy.
He had a sweet ole kind of sweet ole way that did belie
His powers *grands*, his brains *profonds*, his insights *delicettes*,
To whom ze madagascar room was doom; and so he lets
Ze students leave ze desks, and he waves ze big baton,
And lo! ze room is nossing but ze student uny-on!

Hurray! Ze students start to sing! Ze grass
    begins to grow!
And up above ze organ loft where syntax used to blow,
Stands, wizzout no close on, zat nice
    old guy, Rousseau.

Now that the best pizzas in town have been framed
    for the art gallery,
And the slums are selling like hot cakes,
    what shall we eat?
Snipe, dear soul, snipe.

First we must catch one.
Long woolen jocks, handwarmers, boots
    for the bogs.
It is raining, raw nature doth sing
Of the snaring of snipe in the spring.

And so we
Stalk it, salt its tail, ring its bloody neck,
And eat it.
Are you fed now, Soul? Are you whole?

THE SICK ONES

DIALOGUE ONE

Pavlov, that Russian . . .

> Who wants to talk about Pavlov?
> Not I.
> I want to talk about us.

Pavlov loved to talk of the "cerebral hemispheres" . . .

> Did he love?
> Did that man love?

It's a phrase that in English has a pleasant ring
If you let the meaning go, and the connotations.
The connotations in Pavlov are dogs, and a few cats,
With their cerebral hemispheres missing. Their
   presence is needed,
Pavlov showed.

> And my presence.
> Is my presence needed?

Yet he didn't want the importance that he attached to them
To be taken out of lab context.
He was a physiologist, not a mind man. The word "mind"
He thought a distraction.

> I feed the children, clean the kitchen,
> Make the beds, water the plants,
> Move the furniture, paper the walls.
> Where am I in all this?
> I am losing my mind.

First he performed a "minor operation."
He moved the opening of the salivary duct from in to out.
Then he took the dogs and hung them in harnesses, loosely,
The rest is history.
Drop by drop he measured saliva. Twenty-five years.

  Fifteen years.

DIALOGUE TWO

The creatures in comedies are conventionally creatures
  of habit.
In the middle they stray from their habits, and
  that is a joke.
At the end they return, and that is happiness.
The joking and happiness cease when straying persists,
And that is tragedy. Blandly the genres affirm habits.

  Blandly in genre, in habit
  We sit dying.

The artist may go to his genre as to a lab,
Hang his bitch in a harness and other unspeakables.
Comes quitting time he goes home,
Frets not that his powers are overthrown,
And goes to his bed undisturbed to pick up his tyrannies
In the morning.

  Let us talk about quitting time.
  Shall we talk?
  And other unspeakables?

The bitch hangs there all night, many nights, poor thing,
But when he is done with her,
When he cuts her down and pats her and opens the door,
She must out and bark and wag tail like the other dogs,

36

Or he's hung, the artist.
Who's in charge? Not he, not the lab,
But the other dogs.

> Are you done with me?
> Shall we talk? Shall we live?
> And other unspeakables?
> Could we live with the other dogs?

DIALOGUE THREE

There's a brook that I walk to daily,
The mind's choice.

> We could walk together.

When the mosquitoes let me, I stop at it.
I'm building a dam.

> We could build together.

It's two feet across.
I add a few stones each time.

> I could add.

The water keeps going through it
As if it weren't there,
But I keep at it,
Filling the crevices,
My mind's dam.

> Yours always, not ours.

The dam I don't care for.
I'd not take it home.
The first chipmunk could have it.
All I want is to walk there,

Deliberately,
And pick up the stones,
And put in the stones,
And fill in the crevices,
I the determiner,
Tyrant of stones.

Am I a stone?

DIALOGUE FOUR

Let me tell you a story.

I feed the children, clean the kitchen,
Make the beds, water the plants . . .

Will you hear the story?

Will you make it romantic,
Long and romantic
With a happy ending?

I'll tell it,
You be the critic.

I'll be the critic,

Once in a wood walked a tyrant,
Known in the trade as *E*,
Surrounded by *S*s.

What was the trade?

Any tyrant trade.
He walked there, heir of the ages,
Heir of all knowers,
Of witches and wizards —

— and warlocks?
Can the critic supply warlocks? —

— and prophets and poets and sages,
All these and a few kings —

    — and queens,
    Though they didn't know much —

— and old crones —

    — I'll be the critic —

— and rainmakers —

    — and medicine men —

— and philosophers —

    — and alchemists —

— and astrologers —

    — and gurus —

— of course gurus.
All these he was heir to.
He was soft and plump
With a round head.

    He was round and plump
    With a soft head.

He had short legs and short arms,
But long, strong, delicate fingers —

    — like Dr. Kildare.

He was better than Dr. Kildare.

39

But plumper.

With his strong delicate fingers
And his strong analytical mind
And his wood-lore —

    — like Dr. Dolittle —

— and his artist's sense
Of order, pattern, control —

    — call him anal —

— he came to the woods kingly.
In a flash the woods knew him.
He walked under the pines
And the pines stilled.
He held birds in his hands
And the birds did not defecate.
Chipmunks also he held —

    — and they did not defecate —

— and they loved him.

    Dr. Dolittle.

He was fine, this *E*,
Marvelous with his *S*s,
A proper heir
Of sages, prophets, rainmakers,
Poets, wise men, astrologers —

    — and gurus.

Except he kept thinking,
If only these woods,
If only one man in these woods

40

Could bring order
To these woods —

> — and he knew the man.

He knew the man.

> Did he know the girl?
> Where is the girl?
> Surely this movie
> Has a girl.

No girl.
None of his kind.

> Less than kind.

The more he heard of their secrets —

> — secrets? —

— political secrets, social secrets,
Secrets of rot, corruption,
Injustice, slavery.
The more he heard,
The more did the worm creep in him,
The worm of reform.
He would train the woods!

> Hip, hip.

He would rub the lichen off boulders —

> — give the pill to the birds —

— plant the trees in rows —

> — sweep up the pine needles —

41

— bury the dead —

    — bury the girl —

— there was no girl.

    The king of the woods was a liberal and anal,
    An all-American lab man.

So with his strong delicate fingers —

    — he began to pry.
    Can I tell it?

You tell it.

    When the son of a bitch
    Went after their private parts,
    They disowned him.

Worse. They held a meeting.

    The chipmunks?

Chipmunks, ferns,
Bees, pines,
Phoebes, spiders,
Woodchucks —

    — this is too long.

They met.
They stormed, they plotted.
"Get the tyrant,"
Shouted a hawk —

    — and a dove sighed.

"String him up,"

Cried a small tarantula —

    — and a girl clapped.

There was no girl.

      I do tire
      Of this story.

And they moved in.
And there was *E*,
Trapped, as it appeared,
By his own *S*s.
He looked around him,
Looked in the eyes,
And his own drooped.
He squinted ahead of him,
Squinted at paws,
And his fingers slackened.

      The strong, delicate fingers?

All the muscles slackened.
He went limp.
He could move nothing.
He lay on the pine needles.
He looked at the sky.
He tried to speak,
But his voice was silent.

      The chipmunks had got him!

And the ferns, and the bees,
They had got him, he the determiner,
Except —

      — with a shriek of compassion

The girl entered the woods.

Call it that.

Call it that?

He began to sing.

But his voice was silent.

Mi-mi-mi, he whispered.
Mi-mi-mi, and the voice swelled.
Mi-mi-mi- —

— and the girl helped him up,
And they made their way through the chipmunks,
Slowly, out of the woods
Into the meadow,
Where they made the scene
Until quitting time.

You're the tyrant.

What, then, critic?

The song only,
And maybe not that.

Can we both sing the song?

Let us both sing the song.

NOTE: There is a disease, myasthenia gravis, to which E's
trouble loosely conforms. In laboratory experiments E
stands for experimenter, S for subject.

THE TERRIBLE FLAT PEOPLE

See, they return,
The flat people.
They are flat, they have two dimensions,
Not three.
See, they return
From the library shelves
Where the three-dimensional
People put them!

How simple they are, how predictable,
And terrible.
They are types (ugh); they are characters
Walking the earth
With labels across their chests — dean, landlord,
Fuzz, racist (ugh);
And now they are sitting
Where the three-dimensional
People sat!

(Or so say the papers,
Flatly.
Hear the flatulence.)

So now the three-dimensional
People are sitting complexly
Elsewhere.
They are feeling (with mixed feelings)
Thinner.
Fascists!
Henchmen of Wall Street!
                              — see how they shrink,
The well-rounded (ugh)
People.

"The tree is lazy. It wastes time.
I am lazy. I waste time.
So I must be
A tree," said the rock.

"No, you rock," said the bird,
"Try again."

"The tree is lazy. I'm a rock.
I must not be
Lazy," said the rock.

"That's better," said the bird.

"I may be lazy,"
Said the tree,
"But I'm no tree.
I'm a birch."

"They talk so stupidly,"
Said the man,
And rammed into the lazy rock birch bird tree.

A FASCINATING POET'S DIARY

I am keeping this diary because I am fascinating.
My impacted wisdom teeth are fascinating.
My diet, my sex life, my career, these also are
    fascinating,
As are my newspaper clippings. Fascinating.
And all in my little book.

Up to now I have stuck to fascinating
    facts in my book,
Starting at six A.M. when I rise, shave, and
    write in my book,
And ending at ten-thirty when I retire with
    Agatha Christie and my book;
But starting today I propose to include fascinating
    dreams in my book.
In fact I have just had a smasher
In which I find myself wearing a fascinatingly
    old-fashioned six-button book.

Oh little book, oh sweetie, how you adorn me!

METAMORPHOSIS

The little self and the big self walked in a wood,
As in a play.
The big self was wary; he knew that the wood
Did dabble in selves in its pastoral way.

But the little self, the child,
Little knowing the trying and testing of selves by woods,
Lusted for sylvan simplicities, and said to the big self,
"Man, could I buy these goods?"

So the big self, very mature, said he'd have to ponder,
And excused himself and went and sat in an empty spot,
And looked high in the pine trees and low in
    the pine roots,
And returned at length and queried, "How much
    have you got?"

The child allowed he had ten or twelve bucks in
    his pocket
For such woodland wild —
To whom should he make his offer? And the big
    self murmured,
"To the child, child."

JUICE

We number two or three hundred
Million. We are hungry. We sit in the coffee shop waiting.
Why do the trains and pipelines not serve us the breakfast?

I look at my neighbor.
He has a cardiac face and four small children.
The children are spilling the water.
The mother is whispering threats, pinching their biceps.

                            What should we do?

But now they are bringing the orange juice.
I catch the eye of my neighbor. He is smiling, drinking
   his orange juice.
The children are drinking. They have lovely drinkings.
   The mother is drinking. Even I am drinking.

Neighbor,
We will see this through.
We will make it to lunch.

It was a big boxy wreck of a house
Owned by a classmate of mine named Rod Usher,
Who lived in the thing with his twin sister.
He was a louse and she was a souse.

While I was visiting them one wet summer, she died.
We buried her,
Or rather we stuck her in a back room for a bit,
    meaning to bury her
When the graveyard dried.

But the weather got wetter.
One night we were both waked by a twister,
Plus a screeching and howling outside that
    turned out to be sister
Up and dying again, making it hard for Rod to
    forget her.

He didn't. He and she died in a heap, and I left
    quick,
Which was lucky since the house fell in right after,

                              Like a ton of brick.

With wrinkles gathering, gathering round the eyes
And the flesh, as beauticians say, losing its tone,
It is time to sit and be wise,
Rather than loving, carousing, and getting brown.

No more of all that riot. No more gaudy
Egyptian nights. Let books and puzzles
Reign. Let bad old bawdry
Live with a college boy who flames and guzzles.

The flab, flab, flab will then go firm.
The creases will be ironed out by Mind.
The eyes for age on age will brightly burn,
Powered by the dry cells behind.

A DREAM OF AN ATTIC

In a dream I find in an attic my two brothers,
And my own son, and I hear shouting,
One brother ordering other out of the attic,
Other declining,
And I wake and walk to my studio through the woods
With my flashlight, some jelly rolls, and
    these dream goods.

No moon, no wind. Like an attic. But where?
I run through old attics in darkness.
    None of them fits.
None of them has the look of the dream,
    nor the presence
Unnameable in it that now I have lost
On the road in the night with my jelly
    rolls, dream-crossed.

So I come to my desk with my mystery and sit down
And think of all beginnings in all attics
With brothers and sons there, and the shouting,
And I see that the part of dream that
    I couldn't know
On the road in the night with the jelly rolls
Was I. Where did I go?

A TREE IN D.C.

Bare has been bare
For the crooked old tree
By my second-floor study
In D.C.
Since the first year
In the wordy Welsh air
Of its infancy.

A scholar tree,
It knows gnarled to be
From the German for hard and lumpy;
But is senile, thinking the clumsy nest
In its branched fork in the mist
Is to flee to and sit down in
For an old Roman.

It is rooted and weathered to fixity.
It feels not the outer wintry.
Its own nearly speechless cold
Is within, and back, and down,
And at least twice as old
As the German.

It is my word tree,
The living bone,
Writing its own
Mythic but lonely
History.

GUARD:

    Where does it go, go, that high rhetoric,
    When it skims over the heads and soars to the balcony,
    And flaps at the stained-glass windows, verily?

TRILOBITE:

    No energy is lost. The vast abyss
    Steams with the fallout breathed since Genesis.

THINKING OF TENTS

I am thinking of tents and tentage, tents through the ages.
I had half a tent in the army and rolled it religiously,
But Supply stole it back at war's end, leaving me tentless.
And tentless I thankfully still am, a house man at heart,
Thinking of tents as one who has passed quite beyond tents,
Passed the stakes and the flaps, mosquitoes and mildew,
And come to the ultimate tent, archetypal, platonic,
With one cot in it, and one man curled on the cot
Drinking, cooling small angers, smelling death
   in the distance —
War's end —
World's end —
Sullen Achilles.

MOUNTAINS

Surrounded by mountains I feel I should do mountains.
I buy postcards of them and climb them and eat on them,
And stand on their edges and stare out dutifully from them
At other mountains, thinking of bad art.
Like that, mountains are dumb, not smart.

They are heavy, for heavy poets decked out in gloom,
Who look for the good and the true in the cold
        and the bare,
And think of readers as flats over whom they may loom,
Beetle and tower, hour on hour.
Like them, mountains beetle less than they bore.

Why do we color mountains rather than weigh them?
Not White, not Green, not Blue, not Black,
But Hulking Mountains, Hefty, Hegelian Mountains
We should call them, or High Church Hills.
Like poets, mountains should go on reducing pills.

On the checkerboard of the city the wizard, urban, ponders.
He is GREEN. He sits next to RED and OLIVE.
He owns a small basic industry, two high-rise rental
  apartments, and a shopping center.
Each is a square mile.
On each he earns twenty percent per annum not
  counting taxes.
He owns the mayor and two councilmen. They are
  against taxes.
He is buying vacant lots in the suburbs to house
  future employees.
He plans to double the gross of the industry and set up
  a mile-square warehouse.
He watches months pass on the wall. He is thirsty.
The computer is on the fritz. LAVENDER is borrowing.
What is SALMON plotting? And PURPLE? He shuffles
  his papers.
His is a city of papers and paper plots. Nobody
  lives there.
The economy thrives and languishes. Acts of God
  are ten percent,
Riots ten percent, birth and death balanced, not a factor,
Nor love. It is December.

The bell rings.

End of the game.

ON READING S. S. VAN DINE
IN THE CANNED GOODS SECTION

It could be said that there were none of the makings
    of a great detective in S. S. Pierce.
At the scene of the crime the D.A. and the Police
    Chief paid no attention to Pierce,
Who always sat quietly in a corner eating
    applesauce.
The analysts swirled around the corpse,
While Pierce sat there eating.

He asked no questions. He took no measurements.

Yet when the coroner noted a strange sticky
    substance behind the victim's left ear,
And the substance was hastily shipped off to the
    lab, Pierce was always ahead of them all, saying
"It's applesauce." He was right, too, every time.

Each day the earlier dark,
Each dark the strengthened cold.
Blame the fat Utility, blame rich Oil,
Blame the Old,

Those profiteers of winter.

Say, "Thou hast played most foully for it —
For Glamis, Cawdor, All."
Say the sun is rigged, and the jet stream.
Blast City Hall,

Kiddo.

Confront, refute, confound, conspire,
And in your turn shake a leg
To convert the cold to profit,
The dark to a nest egg.

Yes, my America.

For each green fang and claw
Let the season's loot be spread,
As each day the winter widens,
And rude sons strike rude fathers

Dead.

What with the sickness,
The natives,
The Charter's defects, and the King's
Meddling, things
From the start went badly for Company stockholders.

But staunchly they squandered. They had been
Dazzled by biblical images
Of gems, silks, salves and golden elephants,
All manner of Eastern marvels; and so in their parlors
They read the reports of winter on top of winter
Of nothing but debits
(And always the unhappy losses of personnel)
Calmly,
Seeing themselves as patriots who for hard cash
Soon would barter their martyrdoms.

                                        Years
Passed, thus, and the futures
On many a promising item like glass or iron
Slipped from the business pages, leaving
Tobacco, only tobacco, and even that
Pressured by Spanish exports — but still, in those parlors,
Reading the tragic reports, counting their shares,
Drawing up plans for manors in Sussex, and smoking,
The brave stockholders clung to their holdings and swelled
Churchillian chests
With more pounds to invest.

But in Jamestown proper,
Somewhere along the line the original impetus

Blew itself out or was stopped by an Indian arrow
Or something, and suddenly
The gems, silks, salves and golden elephants
Vanished, leaving
A bare but tractable land and a new kind of
Stock.

THE BRUTE

"All the great dangers threatening humani-
ty with extinction are direct consequences
of conceptual thought and verbal speech."
— KONRAD LORENZ

So he conceives,
And in the conceiving
Threatens,
And in the speaking of the conceiving
Threatens.

He is a small man
With a bald head.
He is frightened by spiders.
Neat, he aspires
To a clean desk.
His notes are cross-indexed.
He is shy with females.

But when he conceives
The words come,
And the words are shaped
Like cudgels, like bullets,
Like bombs, like battleships.

He is a small man.
He likes gardening.
He has developed
An exotic mum.

THE LOVERS

Together they stand in the checkout line with
their carton of raspberries.
They are in love. They love raspberries.
He is tall and blond. She is tall and blonde. They
nuzzle each other noisily, exhibitionists in the market,
Surrounded by lesser flesh, envious, purchasing slag.
Soon they will exit, gods into the parking lot,
And drive away in their car with the flowers on it.

But the raspberry season is over and they have chosen
The frozen. The line is long and the carton is
starting to drip.

The future was fuzzy, cold, remote — nothing to touch
    or look at,
Except in *Popular Mechanics*. The past was solid. Waking
    or sleeping he had it, owned it,
As in the den over the bar where his wife had hung a
    rugbeater with a hickory handle.
Called a Batwing Beater. Made in Pennsylvania.
    Handsome gadget.
Simple, decorous. Needed no rug to beat, or bats,
    to earn its keep.
Was it a genuine early American Pennsylvanian antique?
    It didn't matter.
What mattered was that it hung there, had hung there,
    and to the extent that it would hang there
Would do very nicely for a future, thank you, that
    rugbeater.

It hung next to a group of retired candlesticks,
    with dents in them, that had belonged to his mother.
Underneath were the newcomers, the bottles. They came
    and went, nervous things, no stamina,
Except for the lucky ones his wife made into lamps.
The busy ones sat gloomily with their revenue stamps,
Had a job and did it, spent themselves and were done —
    not reformers!
If there was anything in the bloody world he disliked,
    as he sat alone in the bloody world in his rocking chair,
Reformers were it. He locked his doors so they'd not
    get his rugbeater.

But secretly from behind doors he would peer at them
    as they passed,
And in his dreams he cried at the doors, no no,
    in a whisper,
As if some openness tiptoed in him unbolting, unbuttoning.
His wife fretted about him in her sewing room, good woman.
She was making a cover for the rugbeater.

OTHER

The other of man is woman, of lion lamb;
And then there is youth of age, of servant lord,
And so forth.

I have many others,
Like Edgar, Stan, Sterling, Stewart, Smithers.
They walk around me in drugstores and
    bus stations,
Otherly.

What is otherness?

I keep reading in books that deep in the
    drugstores man
Is his own other,
And the bearded shadows are his,
And the thumbed paperbacks.

THE DESK

I sit here at this littered desk, naked,
Looking at me.
Here is the body, there the work. It is morning.
I need a woman to clean me,
Putting the cigarette butts in the wastebasket,
Stacking the letters, dusting me.

I am soiled laundry, unmade beds. What will come of me?
Call the plumber, get him up here,
And the rest of them. What will come of me?

Why does one have to be old and corrupt and messy?
I say tear down firetraps, burn hovels,
Lest they go on for pages, naked and sad.